Times Tables
Activity Book

for ages 5-7

This CGP book is bursting with fun activities to build up children's skills and confidence.

It's ideal for extra practice to reinforce what they're learning in primary school. Enjoy!

Published by CGP

Editors:
Adam Bartlett, Michael Bushell, Ruth Greenhalgh, David Ryan and Joseph Shaw

Proofreading:
Gail Renaud and Glenn Rogers

With thanks to Jan Greenway for the copyright research.

ISBN: 978 1 78908 525 9

Graphics used on the cover and throughout the book © www.edu-clips.com
Cover design concept by emc design ltd.

Printed by Elanders Ltd, Newcastle upon Tyne.

Text, design, layout and original illustrations © Coordination Group Publications Ltd. (CGP) 2020
All rights reserved.

Photocopying this book is not permitted, even if you have a CLA licence.
Extra copies are available from CGP with next day delivery • 0800 1712 712 • www.cgpbooks.co.uk

Contents

Two Times Table	2
More Two Times Table	4
Five Times Table	6
More Five Times Table	8
Ten Times Table	10
More Ten Times Table	12
Puzzle: History Mystery	14
Mixed Problems 1	16
Three Times Table	18
More Three Times Table	20
Four Times Table	22
More Four Times Table	24
Mixed Problems 2	26
Answers	28

Two Times Table

How It Works

Here is the two times table. You can use the sets of dots to help you count to each number in the two times table:

1 × 2 = 2
2 × 2 = 4
3 × 2 = 6
4 × 2 = 8
5 × 2 = 10
6 × 2 = 12
7 × 2 = 14
8 × 2 = 16
9 × 2 = 18
10 × 2 = 20
11 × 2 = 22
12 × 2 = 24

You can also use the times table facts to divide, because dividing is the opposite of multiplying.

E.g. **6 × 2 = 12**, so **12 ÷ 2 = 6** and **12 ÷ 6 = 2**

Now Try These

1. Each of the camels below has two humps. Write the number of camels in each picture and then write the total number of humps.

 1 camel
2 humps

 ☐ camels
☐ humps

 ☐ camels
☐ humps

 ☐ camels
☐ humps

2. Cover up the times table above, then answer these:

2 × 2 = ...   6 × 2 = ...

11 × 2 = ...   7 × 2 = ...

3. Four mummies have escaped from their pyramids. Draw lines to match each of the mummies to the correct pyramid.

4. Fill in the answers to these divisions:

12 ÷ 2 = ………   6 ÷ 2 = ………

2 ÷ 2 = ………   18 ÷ 2 = ………

14 ÷ 2 = ………   22 ÷ 2 = ………

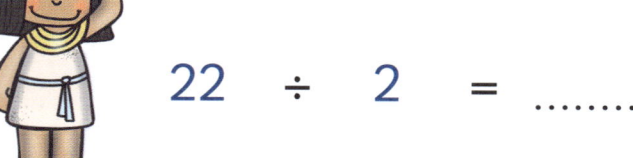

An Extra Challenge

Shade in all the numbers that are in the two times table to help Amelia find a path to the lost tomb.

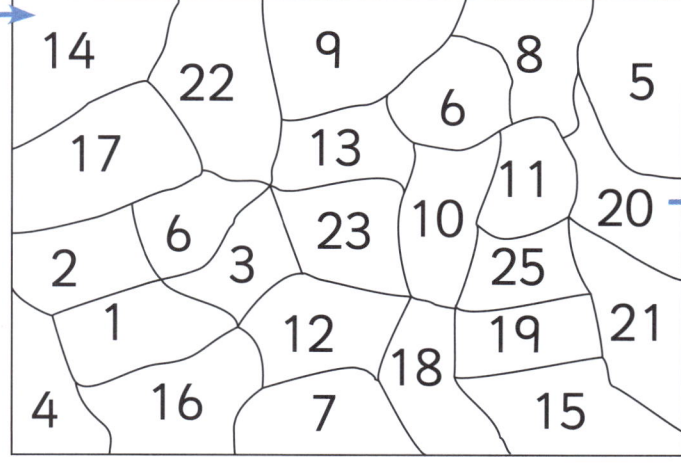

How did you do? Are you too good at the two times table?

More Two Times Table

How It Works

Swapping the order of numbers you are multiplying gives the **same answer**:

What is 2 × 4?

2 × 4 is the same as 4 × 2.
4 × 2 = 8, so 2 × 4 = 8 too.

You can use this to **solve problems** where the numbers are the other way round from in your times table.

Not all two times table problems are written using '×' and '÷'. Sometimes they will be given to you in **words** and you'll need to pick out the numbers:

Vishaal puts **7** blueberries in each muffin that he makes. How many blueberries are there in **2** muffins?

This is asking for **2** lots of **7** blueberries.
2 × 7 is the same as 7 × 2, so 2 × 7 = **14** blueberries.

Now Try These

1. Find how much it would cost to buy:

Two cookies = ... p   Two gingerbread men = ... p

Two hot chocolates = ... p   Two cupcakes = ... p

2. 5 ice creams have 2 scoops each. How many scoops are there in total?

.... scoops

3. Fill in the missing numbers.

☐ × 2 = 4   ☐ × 2 = 8

7 × ☐ = 14   2 × ☐ = 22

4. a) A chocolate bar has 6 cubes.
      How many cubes are in 2 chocolate bars? ....

   b) Two chocolate bars cost 24p.
      How much does one chocolate bar cost? .... p

5. Fill in the missing numbers.

☐ ÷ 2 = 1   ☐ ÷ 2 = 5

20 ÷ ☐ = 10   6 ÷ ☐ = 2

An Extra Challenge

Fill in the gaps to balance all of the scales below. One has been done for you.

How's it going? Are you finding this a piece of cake?

Five Times Table

How It Works

Here is the five times table:

1 × 5 = 5
2 × 5 = 10
3 × 5 = 15
4 × 5 = 20
5 × 5 = 25
6 × 5 = 30
7 × 5 = 35
8 × 5 = 40
9 × 5 = 45
10 × 5 = 50
11 × 5 = 55
12 × 5 = 60

Remember, you can also use the times table facts to divide.

6 × 5 = 30   so   30 ÷ 5 = 6   and   30 ÷ 6 = 5

Now Try These

1. Each starfish has five arms. How many arms are there in each set in total?

8 fives are ☐

3 fives are ☐

5 fives are ☐

8 × 5 = ☐   ☐ × ☐ = ☐   ☐ × ☐ = ☐

2. Help the seals escape from the polar bear by matching them to their ice hole.

7 × 5   4 × 5   35   60

5 × 6   5 × 12   30   20

3. Multiply the number each whale is saying by five.

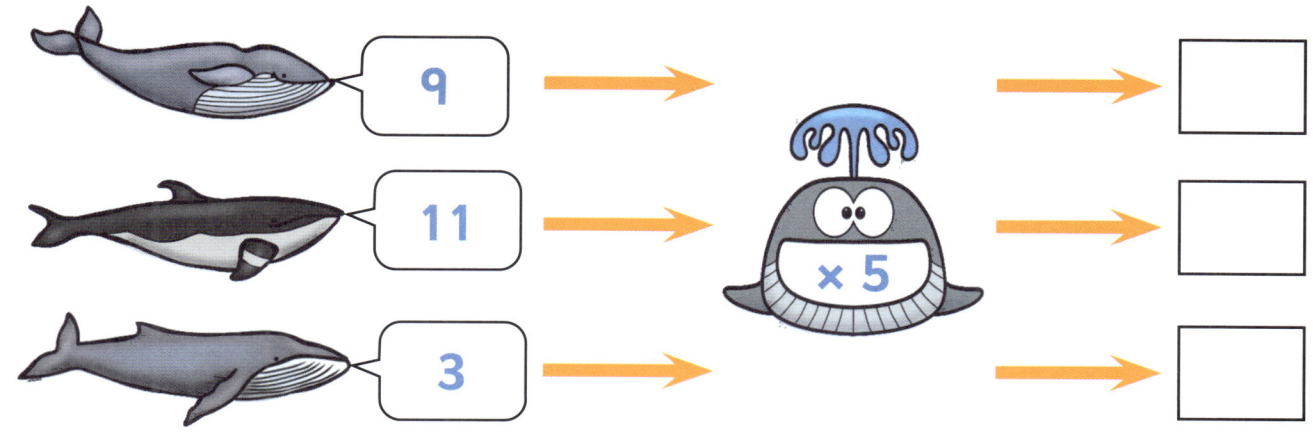

4. Fill in the answers to these divisions.

45 ÷ 5 = ...   20 ÷ 5 = ...

30 ÷ 5 = ...   15 ÷ 5 = ...

An Extra Challenge

Help Harold the hare find a way back through the ice to his burrow. He can only pass over numbers in the 5 times table.

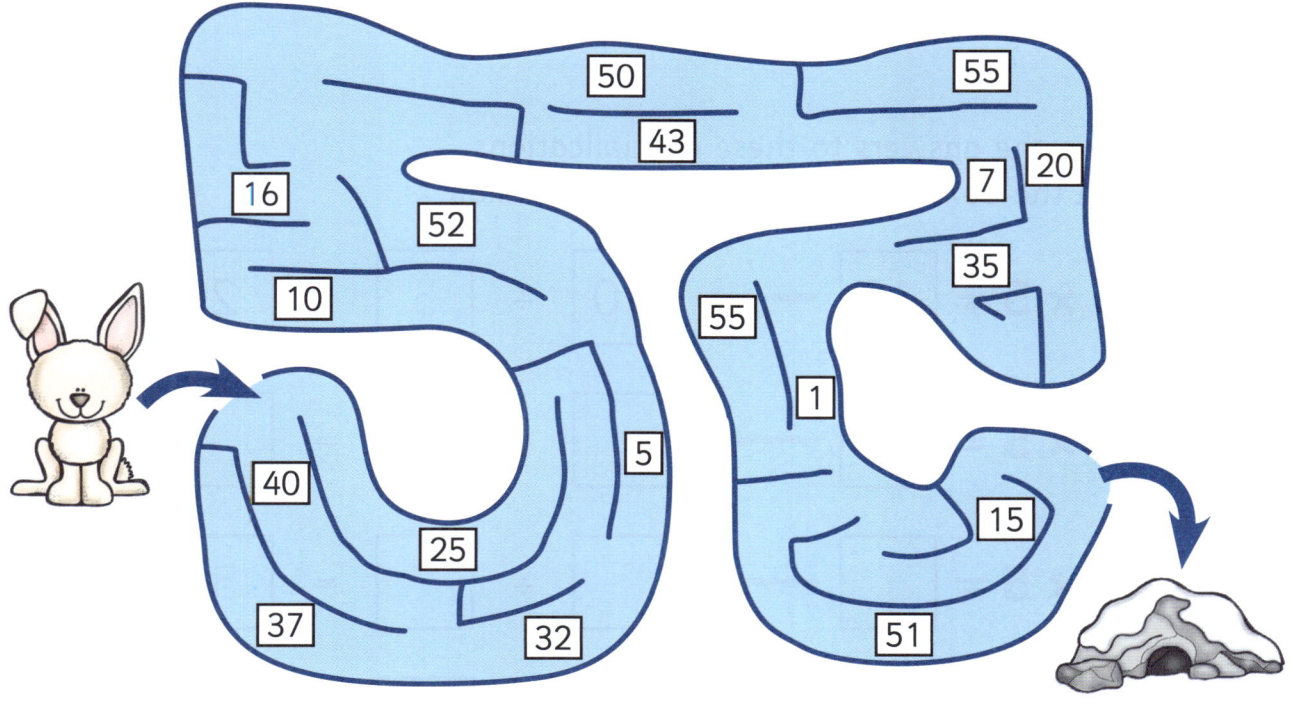

How did it go? Did you do these with no problems?

  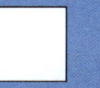

More Five Times Table

How It Works

Take your time when reading a 'wordy' problem so you know exactly what it's asking:

Mindy does **15** dives over **5** days. She does the same number of dives each day. How many dives does she do each day?

This is asking you to share **15** into **5** equal parts.
You need to divide: **15 ÷ 5 = 3** dives each day

Now Try These

1. Sammy the seagull can steal 5 chips with each swoop.
   There are 40 chips in a meal.
   How many swoops does it take Sammy to steal them all?

   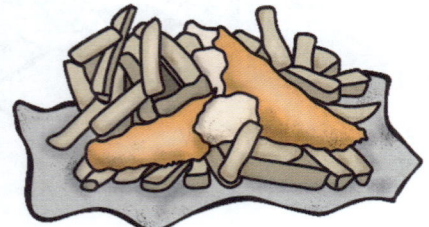   .... swoops

2. Write down the answers to these multiplications.
   Then fill in the boxes to make a matching division.

   2 × 5 = [10] → [10] ÷ [5] = [2]

   9 × 5 = [ ] → [ ] ÷ [5] = [ ]

   7 × 5 = [ ] → [ ] ÷ [ ] = [5]

   11 × 5 = [ ] → [ ] ÷ [11] = [ ]

3. How much would 4 telescopes cost?  £ ....

4. Fill in the missing numbers.

| 5 | × | ☐ | = | 5 |

| ☐ | ÷ | 8 | = | 5 |

| 5 | × | ☐ | = | 50 |

| ☐ | ÷ | 5 | = | 12 |

| 5 | × | ☐ | = | 15 |

| 35 | ÷ | ☐ | = | 5 |

5. Jamil, Sam and Laura each found 5 shells on the beach. How many shells did they find in total?

.... shells

6. A lighthouse flashes 35 times in 5 minutes. How many times does it flash in 1 minute?

.... times

An Extra Challenge

To find the right tank for each fish, divide the number on each fish by five. Draw lines to match each fish to its tank.

What number fish would go in the tank that you haven't matched up? ....

Have you got sea-riously good at the five times table?

Ten Times Table

How It Works

This is the ten times table.

1 × 10 = 10	7 × 10 = 70
2 × 10 = 20	8 × 10 = 80
3 × 10 = 30	9 × 10 = 90
4 × 10 = 40	10 × 10 = 100
5 × 10 = 50	11 × 10 = 110
6 × 10 = 60	12 × 10 = 120

Now Try These

1. Cover up the times table above, then answer these:

   3 × 10 = ...   1 × 10 = ...

   2 × 10 = ...   9 × 10 = ...

   10 × 10 = ...   6 × 10 = ...

2. Draw a ring around each can of paint that has a number that's in the ten times table.

110   55   5   42

24   40   30   20

3. Fill in the answers to the divisions below.

120 ÷ 10 = ...   50 ÷ 10 = ...

20 ÷ 10 = ...   80 ÷ 10 = ...

4. Draw lines to connect each calculation to the painting showing its answer.

10 × 8

      30 ÷ 10

7 × 10

      60 ÷ 10

10 × 9

      120 ÷ 10

An Extra Challenge

Andrea mixes the paint in each box below to make different colours.
There is 10 ml of paint in each tube.
How much paint does she have after mixing each set?

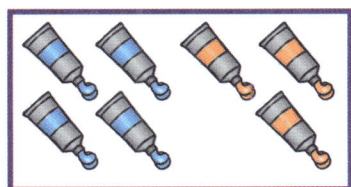 _____ ml   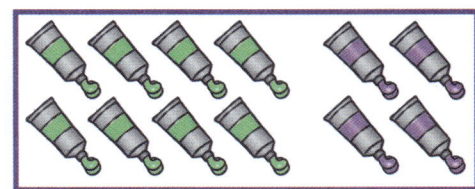 _____ ml

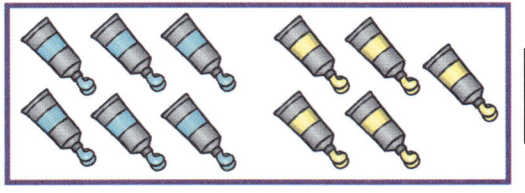 _____ ml

Are you off to a good start with the ten times table?   □   □    □

11

More Ten Times Table

How It Works

It can be tricky to pick out information from wordy problems. Here's an example to help you out:

Eric takes **10** minutes to put up a tent.
How long does it take him to put up **3** tents?

This is asking for **3** lots of **10** minutes.
3 × 10 = 30 minutes

All numbers in the 10 times table end in zero.

Now Try These

1. The images below are labelled with how much each item weighs.

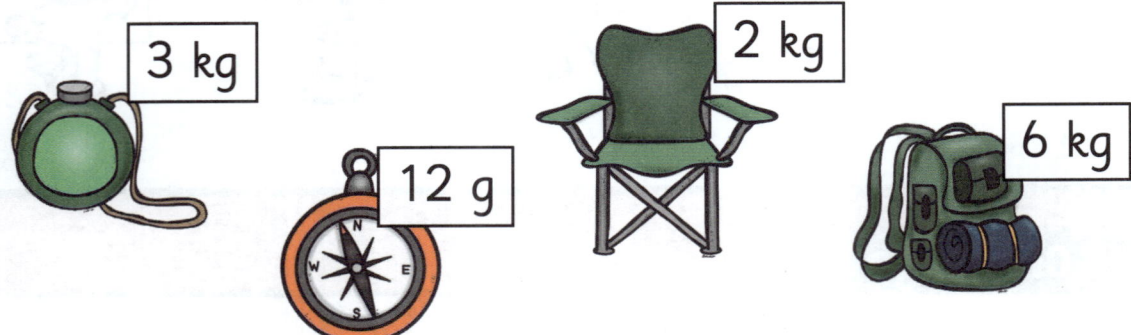

a) How much would 10 compasses weigh in total?   .... g

b) How much would 10 backpacks weigh in total?   .... kg

c) How much would 10 chairs and 10 flasks weigh in total?   .... kg

2. Circle the map that matches the division on the sign.

3. 10 people can fit in a tent.
   How many people would fit in 5 tents?   ………… people

4. How much would 7 cups cost?      £ …………

5. Fill in the missing numbers.

   12 × ☐ = 120   60 ÷ ☐ = 6

   ☐ × 10 = 100   ☐ ÷ 10 = 3

   10 × ☐ = 40   110 ÷ ☐ = 10

6. There are 20 ponies in 10 fields. There are the same number of ponies in each field. How many ponies are there in each field?

………… ponies

An Extra Challenge

Morag is doing a long walk for charity.
Look at what she says below.
How much further does Morag need to walk?

The walk is 2 × 10 miles long.

I have walked 80 ÷ 10 miles already.

How do you feel about the ten times table? All good to go?

13

History Mystery

Travel through history by solving these problems.

The answer to each problem will give you a letter.

Write it in the box at the end to find a word.

1 Find pairs of numbers that multiply together to give answers between 20 and 26. Join the pairs of numbers with straight lines. What letter have you made?

      3
1   9

2   12

8   7
     15

5 What is the letter on the door that matches the key?

A	E	I
24 ÷ 4	3 × 4	30 ÷ 5

O	U
36 ÷ 4	6 × 3

6 Draw lines along tracks that connect multiplications with answers in the 3 times table.

What letter have you made?

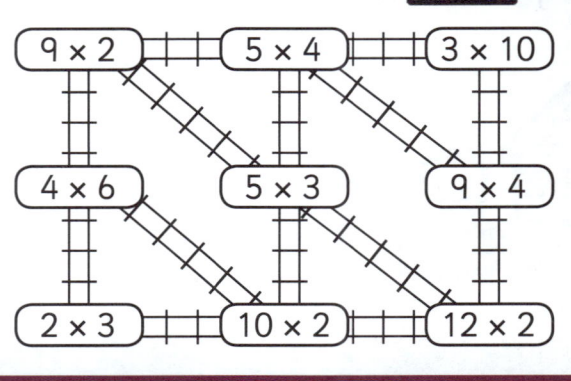

9 × 2   5 × 4   3 × 10
4 × 6   5 × 3   9 × 4
2 × 3   10 × 2   12 × 2

2

🍇 × 2 = 6   so   🍇 = ...

What is the first letter of the number you get when you do:

🍇 × 🍇 = ?

3

Sail over all numbers that 24 can be divided by. 24 can be divided by 2 as 24 ÷ 2 = 12, so start with 2. What letter do you make?

13	12	6	2
30	8	10	20
18	3	7	9
5	4	24	1

Start here

Finish here

4

Which times table do all the numbers on the horses belong to?

Write the second letter of the number.

30   10   15   25

7

Make a letter by shading in all of the numbers in the four times table on the computer screen.

36	12	8	19	21
14	44	34	9	26
5	4	25	42	18
31	28	37	2	46

Answer

1. ....
2. ....
3. ....
4. ....
5. ....
6. ....
7. ....

Mixed Problems 1

How It Works

Some problems won't tell you which times table to use. You may even have to use more than one:

Martha digs up **2** lettuces and **5** carrots every day.
How many of each vegetable does she dig up in **7** days?

This is asking for...

7 lots of 2 lettuces.
7 × 2 = 14 lettuces

7 lots of 5 carrots.
7 × 5 = 35 carrots

Now Try These

1. Fill in the empty circles to finish this number web.
   One has been done for you.

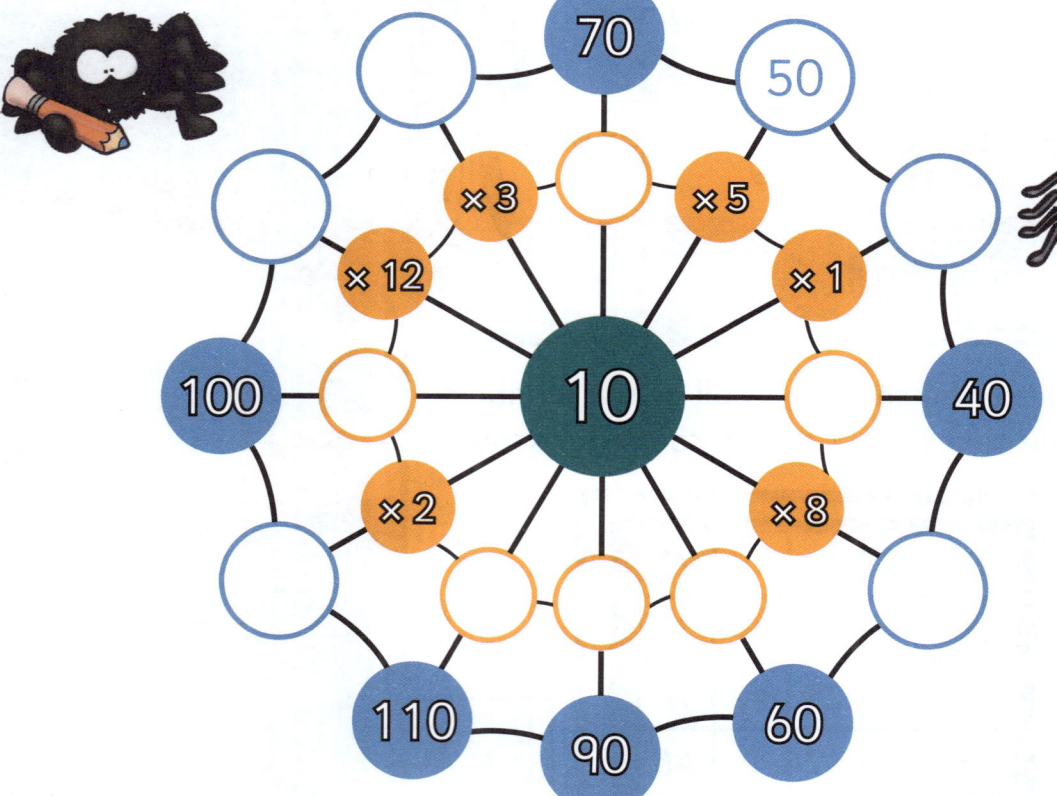

2. A spider has 8 legs.
   How many legs do 2 spiders have?

   .... legs

3. A bird eats 5 seeds each day.
   How many seeds will it eat in 6 days?

   .... seeds

4. Here are the prices of some items.

   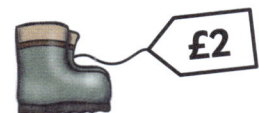  

   Pair of Wellies   Bird House   Wheelbarrow

   How much would it cost to buy the following sets?

   a) 3 wheelbarrows   b) 7 pairs of wellies   c) 12 bird houses

   £ ....   £ ....   £ ....

5. Fill in the missing numbers.

   7 × ☐ = 35   ☐ ÷ 2 = 11

   ☐ ÷ 8 = 10   5 × ☐ = 20

An Extra Challenge

Help Francis the frog get across the pond to meet his friends. Draw a path over the lily pads that only goes through numbers in the 2 or 5 times tables.

Are your times tables coming along in leaps and bounds?

Three Times Table

How It Works

Here is the three times table:

1 × 3 = 3
2 × 3 = 6
3 × 3 = 9
4 × 3 = 12

5 × 3 = 15
6 × 3 = 18
7 × 3 = 21
8 × 3 = 24

9 × 3 = 27
10 × 3 = 30
11 × 3 = 33
12 × 3 = 36

Don't forget, you can also turn times table facts around and use them to divide:

E.g. **6 × 3 = 18**, so **18 ÷ 3 = 6** and **18 ÷ 6 = 3**

Now Try These

1. There are 3 sausages on each plate.
   How many sausages are there on each table?

2. Cover up the times table above, then answer these:

   2 × 3 = ...   6 × 3 = ...

   11 × 3 = ...   7 × 3 = ...

18

3. Match each fork to the knife with the correct answer.
   One has been done for you.

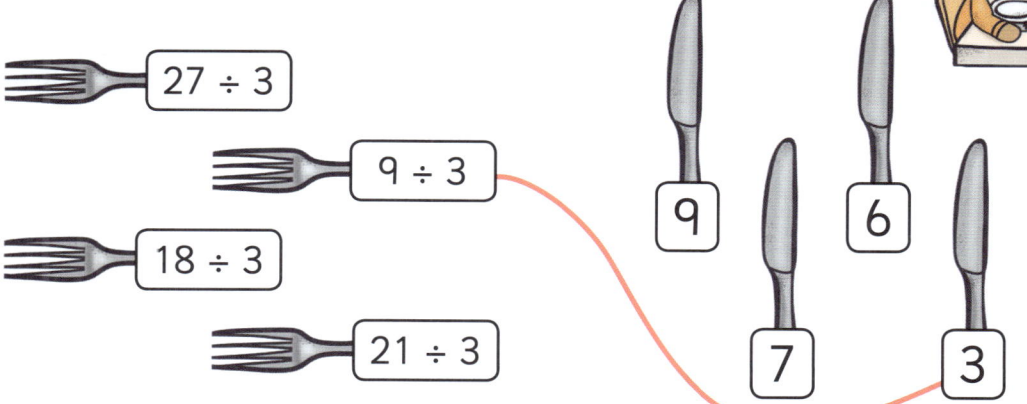

4. Fill in the answers to the divisions below.

$12 \div 3 = $ .... $6 \div 3 = $ ....

$30 \div 3 = $ .... $36 \div 3 = $ ....

An Extra Challenge

Each member of this family has a stool. Their ages are shown on the cards.
The four youngest members sit on the top row of stools.
They sit opposite someone 3 times their age. Where could everyone sit?

Are you feeling good about the three times table?

More Three Times Table

How It Works

Take your time when reading a wordy problem so you know exactly what it's asking:

Phil packs **30** socks into **3** bags. Each bag has the same number of socks. How many socks are in each bag?

This is asking you to share **30** into **3** equal parts. You need to divide: **30 ÷ 3 = 10** socks

Now Try These

1. These vehicles show the cost of 3 tickets. Draw lines to match each vehicle with the cost of one ticket.

 £6

 £36

£2

£5   £12

£7

 £21

 £15

2. Eni goes to 4 countries and stays 3 days in each. How many days did she stay in total?

.... days

3. One plane needs 3 pilots.
   How many planes do 8 planes need?

   .... pilots

4. Fill in the missing numbers.

   3 × ☐ = 6

   ☐ ÷ 8 = 3

   3 × ☐ = 27

   ☐ ÷ 3 = 11

   3 × ☐ = 15

   36 ÷ ☐ = 3

5. There are 27 seats on a plane. Each row has 3 seats.
   How many rows of seats are there?

   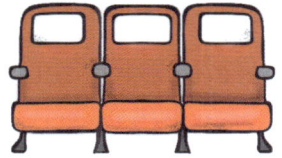 

   .... rows

An Extra Challenge

Shade numbers in the 3 times table to reveal the image.

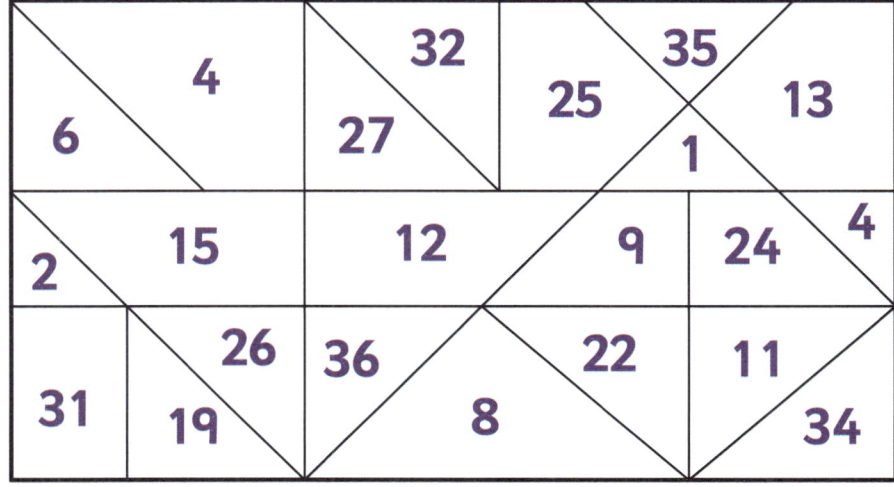

Are you flying high with
the three times table?

Four Times Table

How It Works

Here is the four times table. All the answers in the 4 times table are even — just like the 2 times table.

1 × 4 = 4

2 × 4 = 8

3 × 4 = 12

4 × 4 = 16

5 × 4 = 20

6 × 4 = 24

7 × 4 = 28

8 × 4 = 32

9 × 4 = 36

10 × 4 = 40

11 × 4 = 44

12 × 4 = 48

Now Try These

1. Each bunch has four bananas. How many bananas are there in each set?

3 fours are ☐

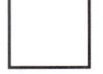 × = ☐

(3 × 4 = ☐)

10 fours are ☐

☐ × ☐ = ☐

7 fours are ☐

☐ × ☐ = ☐

2. Cover up the times table above, then answer these:

4 × 4 = ...

5 × 4 = ...

11 × 4 = ...

8 × 4 = ...

3. Marvin is throwing bananas at a wheel. He only hits numbers in the four times table.

   Draw splats where the bananas hit. One has been done for you.

4. Fill in the answers to the divisions below.

   12 ÷ 4 = ...　　　　36 ÷ 4 = ...

   24 ÷ 4 = ...　　　　48 ÷ 4 = ...

An Extra Challenge

Milly only swings on vines where the leaves add up to a number in the four times table. Tick the vines that she will swing on.

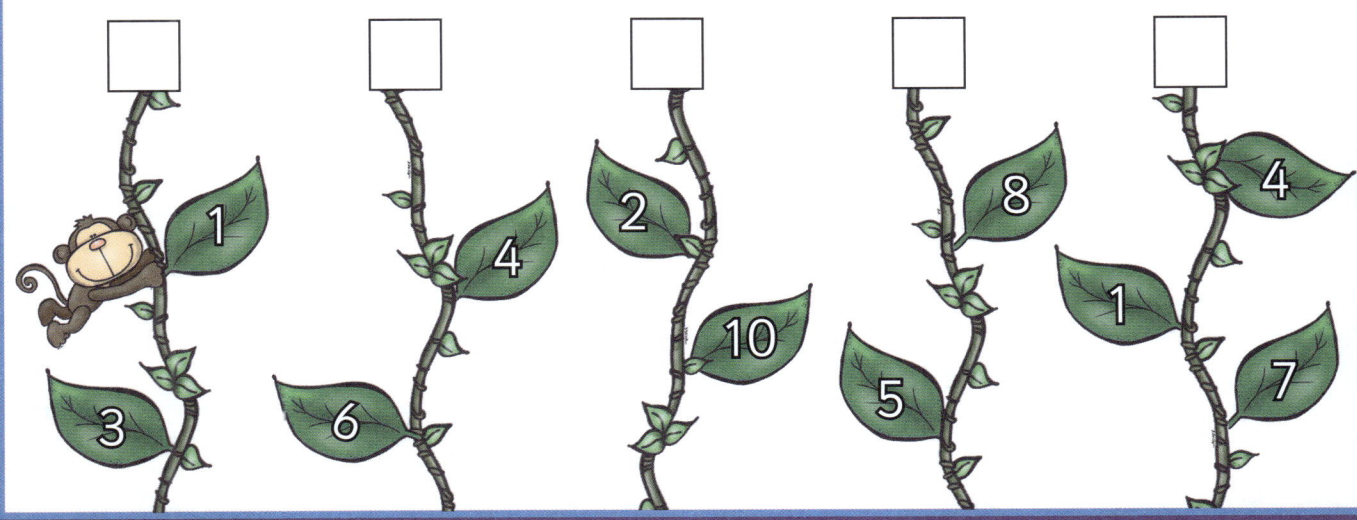

How was that? Did you go bananas for this topic?

More Four Times Table

How It Works

Make sure you understand if a problem is asking for a multiplication or a division before you get started:

A car has 4 wheels.
How many wheels would 12 cars have?

This is asking for 12 lots of 4 wheels.
12 × 4 = 48 wheels

Now Try These

1. These police officers have got their notepads muddled up. Draw lines to match each notepad to the correct officer.

2. A dog wags its tail 4 times in one second. How many times will it wag its tail in 6 seconds?

.... times

3. Children cross the road in groups of 4. 28 children cross the road in total. How many groups is this?

.... groups

4. A magnifying glass makes everything look 4 times bigger. How tall would these objects look?

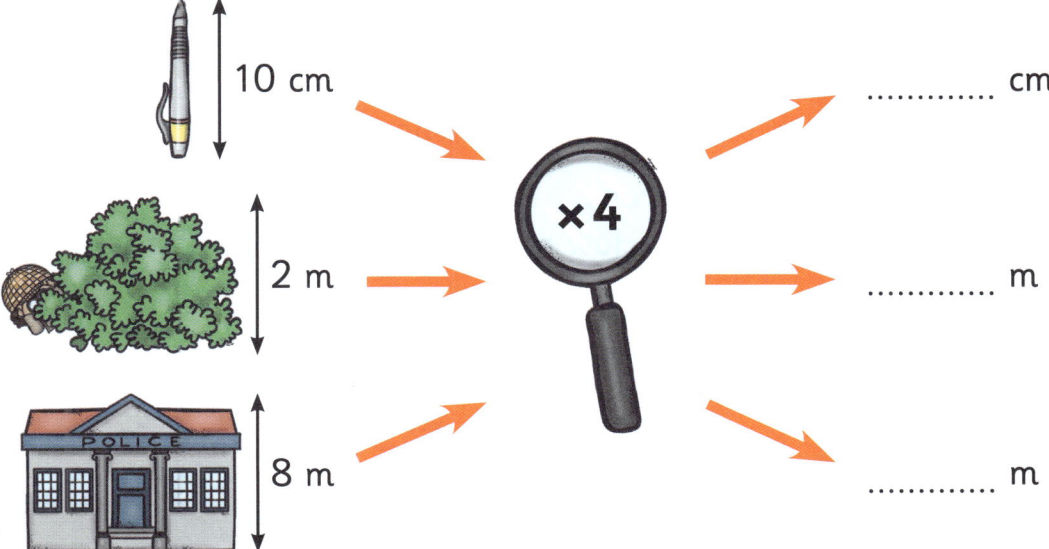

10 cm → .... cm

2 m → .... m

8 m → .... m

5. Fill in the missing numbers.

24 ÷ ☐ = 4

☐ ÷ 4 = 3

☐ ÷ 7 = 4

40 ÷ ☐ = 4

An Extra Challenge

Solve the calculations below. Each answer matches up with a letter. Write down the letters to crack the code.

4 × 4   3 × 4   2 × 4   32 ÷ 4   6 × 4   11 × 4   20 ÷ 5   48 ÷ 4

.... E ....

Number	12	24	4	16	44	8
Letter	E	D	N	W	O	L

How did you do? Did you solve these problems?

Mixed Problems 2

How It Works

Think carefully about which times table to use when solving problems.

Every metre they walk, Gretel drops **10** crumbs and Hansel drops **2** pebbles. They walk **8** metres. How many things do they each drop?

 This is asking for...

 8 lots of 10 crumbs.
8 × 10 = 80 crumbs

 8 lots of 2 pebbles.
8 × 2 = 16 pebbles

Now Try These

1. Draw a ring around the house that matches the pig's number on the left.

 **15**  5 × 10  4 × 3  5 × 3

 **24**  12 × 4  8 × 3  6 × 2

 **30**  6 × 5  11 × 3  10 × 4

2. These three bears each want a bowl and a bed that can multiply together to give their numbers. Match a bowl and a bed to each bear.

 14

 33

 40

 8 11 7

 3

 5

 2

3. One cow can be sold for 4 beans.
   How many beans can 6 cows be sold for?

    =  = ... beans

4. A magic beanstalk grows 4 metres every second.
   How tall will it grow in 7 seconds?

   .... metres

5. A lamb eats 3 bundles of hay every day.
   How many bundles does it eat in 5 days?

   .... bundles

An Extra Challenge

Help Red Riding Hood find a way back to her grandma. Don't pass over numbers in the 3 or 5 times tables — there are wolves hiding behind them!

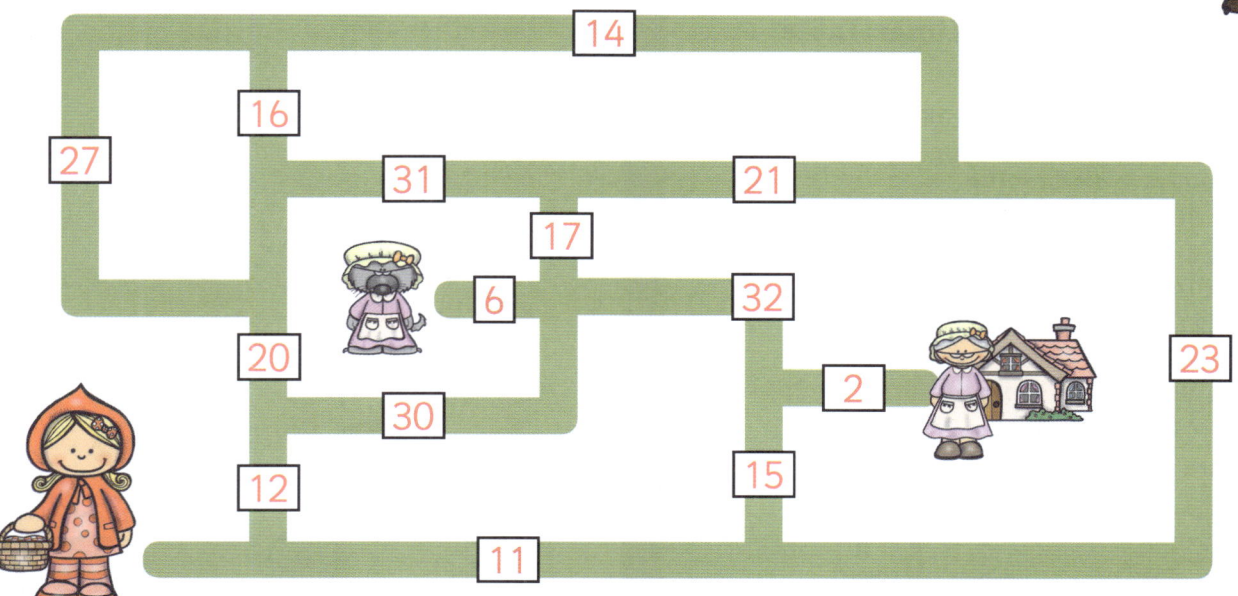

Have your times table skills reached a happy ending?

Answers

Pages 2-3 — Two Times Table

1.  1 camel  3 camels
   2 humps   6 humps

    5 camels  9 camels
   10 humps   18 humps

2. 2 × 2 = 4   6 × 2 = 12
   11 × 2 = 22   7 × 2 = 14

3.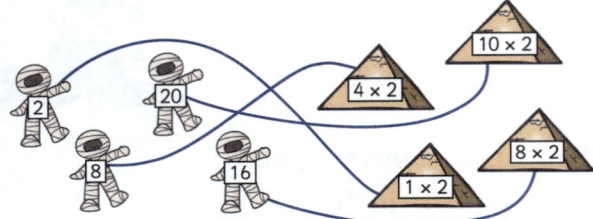

4. 12 ÷ 2 = 6   6 ÷ 2 = 3
   2 ÷ 2 = 1   18 ÷ 2 = 9
   14 ÷ 2 = 7   22 ÷ 2 = 11

An Extra Challenge

 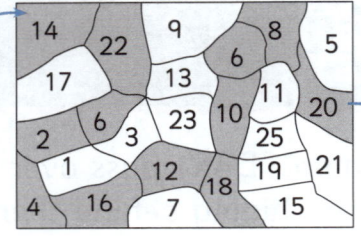 

Pages 4-5 — More Two Times Table

1. Two cookies = 2 × 3p = **6p**
   Two hot chocolates = 2 × 9p = **18p**
   Two gingerbread men = 2 × 7p = **14p**
   Two cupcakes = 2 × 8p = **16p**

2. 5 × 2 = 10 scoops

3. **2** × 2 = 4   **4** × 2 = 8
   7 × **2** = 14   2 × **11** = 22

4. a) 6 × 2 = 12 cubes
   b) 24p ÷ 2 = 12p

5. **2** ÷ 2 = 1   **10** ÷ 2 = 5
   20 ÷ **2** = 10   6 ÷ **3** = 2

An Extra Challenge

Pages 6-7 — Five Times Table

1. 8 fives are 40   3 fives are 15   5 fives are 25
   8 × 5 = 40   3 × 5 = 15   5 × 5 = 25

2.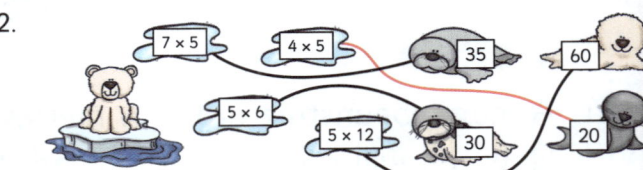

3. 9 → 45
   11 → 55
   3 → 15
   (×5)

4. 45 ÷ 5 = 9   20 ÷ 5 = 4
   30 ÷ 5 = 6   15 ÷ 5 = 3

An Extra Challenge

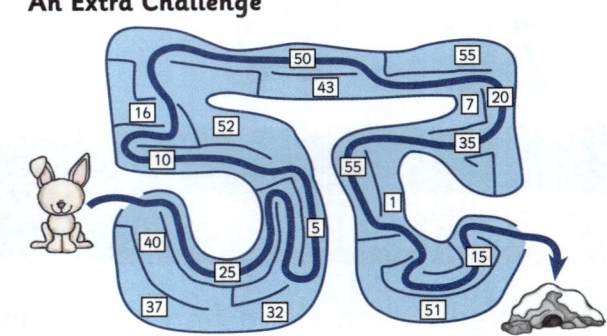

Pages 8-9 — More Five Times Table

1. 40 ÷ 5 = 8 swoops
2. 9 × 5 = **45** → **45** ÷ 5 = **9**
   7 × 5 = **35** → **35** ÷ 7 = 5
   11 × 5 = **55** → **55** ÷ 11 = **5**
3. 4 × £5 = £20
4. 5 × **1** = 5   60 ÷ 5 = 12
   40 ÷ 8 = 5   5 × **3** = 15
   5 × **10** = 50   35 ÷ **7** = 5
5. 3 × 5 = 15 shells
6. 35 ÷ 5 = 7 times

An Extra Challenge

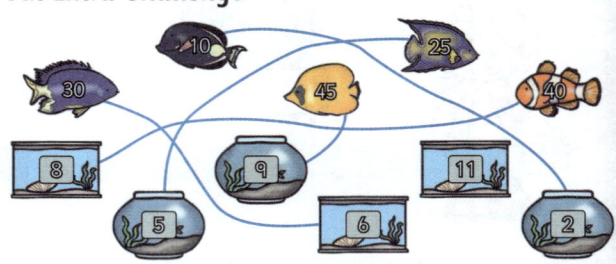

The tank left over is number 11.
Fish number 11 × 5 = 55 would go in tank 11.

Answers

Pages 10-11 — Ten Times Table

1. 3 × 10 = 30   1 × 10 = 10
   2 × 10 = 20   9 × 10 = 90
   10 × 10 = 100 6 × 10 = 60
2.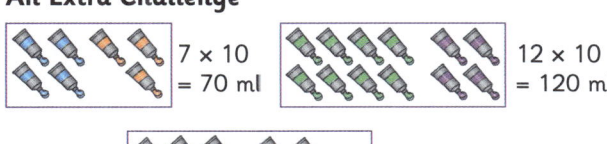
3. 120 ÷ 10 = 12   50 ÷ 10 = 5
   20 ÷ 10 = 2   80 ÷ 10 = 8
4.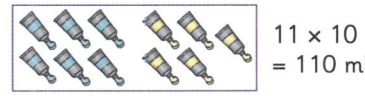

An Extra Challenge

Pages 12-13 — More Ten Times Table

1. a) 10 × 12 g = 120 g
   b) 10 × 6 kg = 60 kg
   c) 10 × 2 kg + 10 × 3 kg = 20 kg + 30 kg = 50 kg
2. (9 circled) 18 20
3. 5 × 10 = 50 people
4. 7 × £10 = £70
5. 12 × **10** = 120   60 ÷ **10** = 6
   10 × 10 = 100   **30** ÷ 10 = 3
   10 × **4** = 40   110 ÷ **11** = 10
6. 20 ÷ 10 = 2 ponies

An Extra Challenge

The walk is 2 × 10 = 20 miles long.
Morag has walked 80 ÷ 10 = 8 miles already.
So there are 20 − 8 = 12 miles left.

Pages 14-15 — History Mystery

1.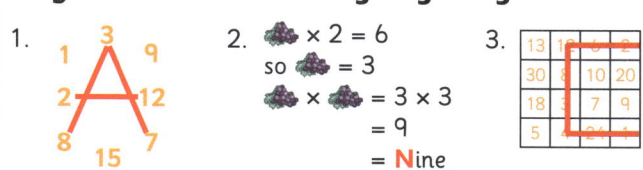
2. 🍇 × 2 = 6
   so 🍇 = 3
   🍇 × 🍇 = 3 × 3
       = 9
       = **N**ine
3. (grid)
4. 30 = 6 × 5, 10 = 2 × 5, 15 = 3 × 5 and 25 = 5 × 5 are all in the f**i**ve times table.
5. E — 3 × 4
6.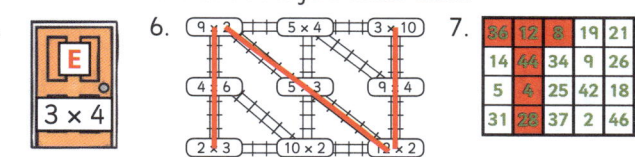
7. (grid)

The word is A N C I E N T.

Pages 16-17 — Mixed Problems 1

1.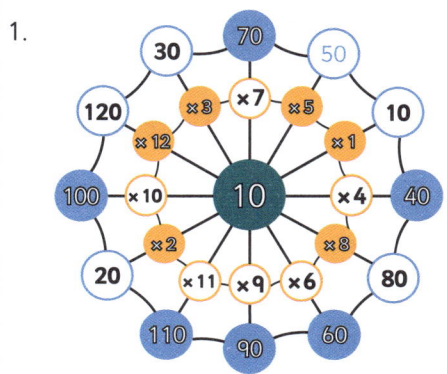
2. 2 × 8 = 16 legs
3. 6 × 5 = 30 seeds
4. a) 3 × £10 = £30   b) 7 × £2 = £14
   c) 12 × £5 = £60
5. 7 × **5** = 35   **22** ÷ 2 = 11
   80 ÷ 8 = 10   5 × 4 = 20

An Extra Challenge

Pages 18-19 — Three Times Table

1. 5 × 3 = 15   8 × 3 = 24
2. 2 × 3 = 6   6 × 3 = 18
   11 × 3 = 33   7 × 3 = 21
3.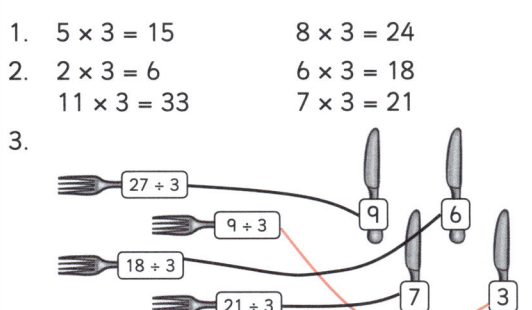

Answers

4. 12 ÷ 3 = 4   6 ÷ 3 = 2
   30 ÷ 3 = 10 36 ÷ 3 = 12

An Extra Challenge

E.g.

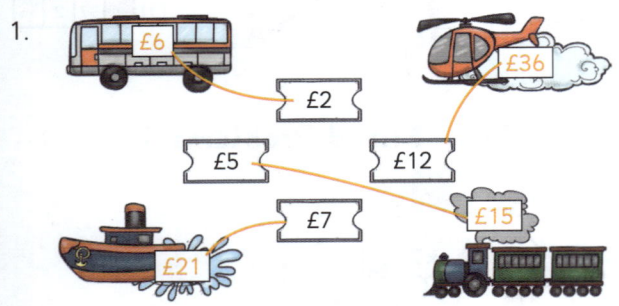

Pages 20-21 — More Three Times Table

1. (bus £6 → £2; helicopter £36 → £12; boat £21 → £7; train £15 → £5)
2. 4 × 3 = 12 days
3. 8 × 3 = 24 pilots
4. 3 × **2** = 6   **33** ÷ 3 = 11
   24 ÷ 8 = 3   3 × **5** = 15
   3 × **9** = 27   36 ÷ **12** = 3
5. 27 ÷ 3 = 9 rows

An Extra Challenge

Pages 22-23 — Four Times Table

1. 3 fours are 12 10 fours are 40 7 fours are 28
   3 × 4 = 12 10 × 4 = 40 7 × 4 = 28
2. 4 × 4 = 16   5 × 4 = 20
   11 × 4 = 44 8 × 4 = 32
3. (wheel: 42, 8, 40, 22, 38, 15)
4. 12 ÷ 4 = 3   36 ÷ 4 = 9
   24 ÷ 4 = 6   48 ÷ 4 = 12

An Extra Challenge
1 + 3 = 4 ✓ 4 + 6 = 10 ✗ 2 + 10 = 12 ✓
8 + 5 = 13 ✗ 4 + 1 + 7 = 12 ✓

Pages 24-25 — More Four Times Table

1.
2. 6 × 4 = 24 times
3. 28 ÷ 4 = 7 groups
4. 10 cm × 4 = 40 cm
   2 m × 4 = 8 m
   8 m × 4 = 32 m
5. 24 ÷ **6** = 4   **28** ÷ 7 = 4
   12 ÷ 4 = 3   40 ÷ **10** = 4

An Extra Challenge
WELL DONE

Pages 26-27 — Mixed Problems 2

1. 15 — 5 × 3 circled
   24 — 8 × 3 circled
   30 — 6 × 5 circled
2.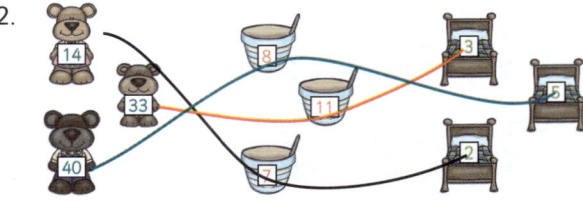
3. 6 × 4 = 24 beans
4. 7 × 4 = 28 metres
5. 5 × 3 = 15 bundles

An Extra Challenge

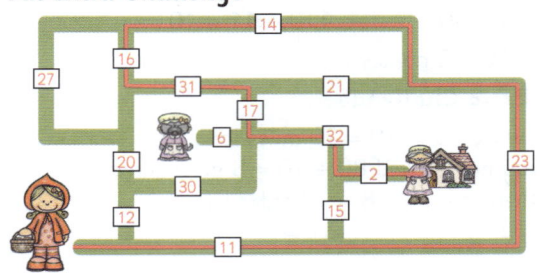